LIFE IN COLONIAL AMERICA

GOVERNMENT IN COLONIAL AMERICA

L.H. COLLIGAN

Cavendish
Square

New York

Published in 2015 by Cavendish Square Publishing, LLC
243 5th Avenue, Suite 136, New York, NY 10016

Copyright © 2015 by Cavendish Square Publishing, LLC

First Edition

Library of Congress Cataloging-in-Publication Data

Colligan, Louise H.
Government in colonial America / by Louise H. Colligan.
p. cm. — (Life in colonial America)
Includes index.
ISBN 978-1-62712-891-9 (hardcover) ISBN 978-1-62712-893-3 (ebook)
1. United States — Politics and government — To 1775 — Juvenile literature. 2. Europe — Colonies — America — Administration — Juvenile literature. 3. United States — Politics and government — To 1775 — Juvenile literature. I. Colligan, Louise H. II. Title.
E188.C65 2015
325—d23

Editorial Director: Dean Miller
Editor: Fletcher Doyle
Senior Copy Editor: Wendy A. Reynolds
Art Director: Jeffrey Talbot
Designer: Joseph Macri
Production Editor: David McNamara
Production Manager: Jennifer Ryder-Talbot

Printed in the United States of America

Contents

INTRODUCTION: Spreading the Word   4

ONE: The Governments Back Home   9

TWO   Origins of Self Government   17

THREE: Government by Charter   23

FOUR: Colonists Start to Pull Away   29

FIVE: Four Hundred Years of Spanish Government   35

SIX: The Government that Came to Stay   47

SEVEN: By the People   57

Glossary   68

Further Reading   72

Quotation Sources   75

Index   78

Author Biography   80

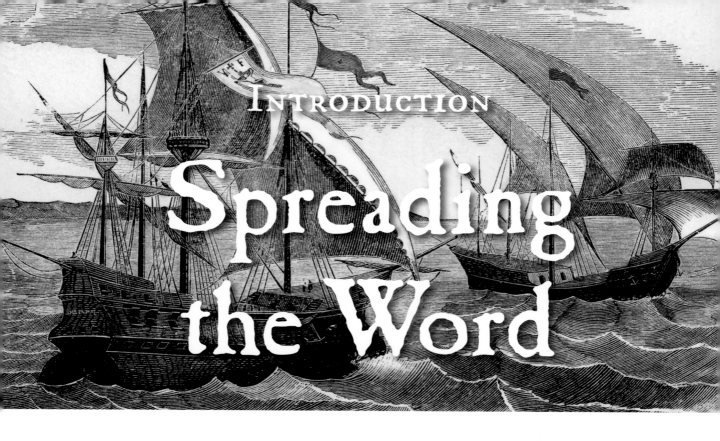

INTRODUCTION

Spreading the Word

I f the printing press had not been invented in 1450, few people in Europe would have learned about Christopher Columbus's voyages to the **New World**. Without the printing press, Columbus himself might not have set off across the Atlantic Ocean in search of faraway lands to conquer for Spain. However, the very year Columbus was born, Johannes Gutenberg did invent a printing press. New information about countries far beyond **Old World** Europe and England became available to many people.

In just a few decades, the small world that ordinary Europeans had known seemed larger. They read that crusaders, who had set out toward Jerusalem to retake the city from Muslim Saracens and to restore safe travel routes for Catholic pilgrims, had opened the Near East to trade. They learned that the Italian merchant,

The invention of the mariner's astrolabe by the end of the fifteenth century made long-distance ocean voyages safer.

Marco Polo, had found riches in Asia to sell in Europe. What other exotic lands might be out there for the taking? European **monarchs** meant to find out.

Portugal and Spain sailed out in search of Asia first. Portuguese sailors headed south around the tip of Africa in 1488. Four years later, King Ferdinand and Queen Isabella of Spain sent Columbus across the Atlantic to find a route to Asia's riches. He thought he had reached India when he landed on the island he called Española. Little did Columbus know that Española lay off the coast of two vast continents, which came to be called **the Americas**. Columbus published an account of his adventures when he returned to Europe.

> This island and all the others are very fertile to a limitless degree, and this island is extremely so. In it there are many harbours on the coast of the sea, beyond comparison with others that I know in Christendom, and many rivers, good and large, which is marvelous ... there are very wide and fertile plains, and there is honey ... In the interior, there are mines of metals, and the population is without number.
> —Christopher Columbus, 1493

Thanks to the printing press, his journals made history. The race to the New World was on. By the early 1500s, explorers such as Giovanni da Verrazano, Henry Hudson, and Hernán Cortéz of Spain travelled well beyond the lands Columbus had visited. In the Western Hemisphere they found oceans, islands, and great continents with millions of people living on them. Unknown to Europeans before 1492, Native Americans had occupied the continents for thousands of years. Many of them lived in societies with organized governments.

Taino chief Guacanagari helped Christopher Columbus build a fort on Española after they met in 1492.

Food availability, territory, and climate determined whether the Native people lived in small, loosely organized groups, or in large ones with structured governments. The early European colonists described the Native American groups they encountered as bands, tribes, and chiefdoms.

BANDS

Hunting and gathering bands lived in small, extended family groups of ten to fifty members who moved from place to place within their territory to forage for food. Because every member participated in feeding the entire group, bands shared power fairly equally. Members used social pressure to keep order.

Many bands did choose one male leader, called a sachem or a sagamore. He dealt with territorial matters and settled disputes within or outside the band. This sachem usually came from a respected family of previous leaders. Bands also valued the experience and advice of their older members as well as their shamans, who were thought to have special powers including the ability to heal the sick. Shamans and elders assisted the leader in solving disagreements by persuasion, not force.

TRIBES

Native Americans who settled in farming villages and hunted seasonally tended to form tribes. Tribal groups were larger than hunter-gatherer bands and more structured in governing themselves. As in bands, everyone in a tribe was involved in food production and shared power and decisions. However, each village within a tribe usually selected a leader called a "headman," as well as a **council** of elders from each family in the tribe. These chosen leaders used persuasion to manage village issues. All tribal members attended council meetings.

CHIEFDOMS AND CONFEDERACIES

Highly structured chiefdoms mainly existed in settled farming areas with rich resources that were under the control of several tribes. Chiefdoms had one chief, who selected council members from each tribe. Overseeing the chief, the council, and all tribal members was a king-like supreme ruler. He had the final word in settling all tribal conflicts and dealing with outsiders.

English colonists encountered confederacies in the Chesapeake Bay area, where tribes had united to deal with incoming settlers. English colonial **governor** George Percy described meeting an impressive **confederacy** chief, called the Werowance, along with the chief's council and protectors in 1607.

> When we landed, the Werowance of Rapahanna came down to the waterside with all his train [attendants], as goodly men as any I have seen of Savages or Christians.
>
> —Governor George Percy, 1607

Native American chiefdoms resembled Old World governments in two ways. Chiefdoms were organized with top-down authority. A powerful leader was the chiefdom's authority figure. He redistributed the group's surplus to those in need. The chief and a small group of noble counselors ruled everyone below them. The chief and the noble counselors inherited their powerful positions. They gained their wealth from the labor of **commoners**. Spiritual leaders, called shamans, belonged to a religious class.

Native Americans formed confederacies to share political power when facing a common enemy or forging peace. Feuds between individual village tribes harmed trade for all groups in an area. Villages joined confederacies to increase their trading power by regulating prices of their goods.

Top-down authority, inherited royal titles and wealth, class divisions, spiritual leaders, and appointed or elected councils were also features of European governments. Yet one group completely dominated the other within a hundred years. By the 1700s, the vital Native American societies of bands, tribes, and chiefdoms were greatly reduced. Most Native Americans were killed by foreign diseases to which they had no protective immunities. Estimates are that between the arrival of Columbus in the Western Hemisphere and the end of the eighteenth century, ninety to ninety-five percent of the Native population had died. As colonists settled in, the weakened bands, tribes, and chiefdoms were no match for the colonial powers. New chiefs, new nobility, new spiritual leaders, and new representatives replaced the old from the Atlantic to the Pacific.

CHAPTER ONE

The Government Back Home

Conquistadors were under royal orders to govern the Spanish colonies with the same laws as those used by the monarchy back home.

Two points are to be observed concerning the right ordering of rulers in a state or nation. One is that all should take some share in the government: for this form of **constitution** ensures peace among the people, commends itself to all, and is most enduring ... Accordingly, the best form of government is in a state or kingdom, where one is given the power to preside over all; while under him are others having governing powers: and yet a government of this kind is shared by all, both because all are eligible to govern, and because the rules are chosen by all.

—St. Thomas Aquinas, 1274

Government by the people and for the people was not the government that Old World Europeans had known in the Middle Ages (from about the fifth through the fifteenth centuries). The ideal three-branch government St. Thomas Aquinas promoted was several hundred years away. Instead, **absolute monarchs** of most European nations ruled from the top with no sharing of power. Beneath the king was a wealthy, landowning **aristocracy**. Below these nobles was a class of males who served in the military. Those who owned small properties belonged to the **gentry**. Church leaders held a privileged position and worked with the royal government to maintain social order. These top social classes made up about five percent of the population. The other ninety-five percent consisted of **peasant** farmers, shopkeepers, artisans, laborers, and the poor. This top-down power pyramid had existed since the beginning of the Middle Ages. It was the only government structure most Europeans had known.

As more printed books became available in the 1400s, Europeans learned that not all people had lived under royal rulers and their lords. In other times and places, such as ancient Greece and Rome, ordinary citizens had participated in democratic governments. People read that Greek and Roman governments were far more open than their own. Those who had been ruled by monarchs and church authorities must have found this Greek historian's "power-to-the-people" idea eye-opening:

> Again, it is the people who bestow offices on the deserving, which
> are the most honourable rewards of virtue. It has also the absolute power
> of passing or repealing laws; and, most important of all, it is the people who
> deliberate on the question of peace or war.
> —Polybius, *Histories*, ca. 150 BCE

Greek philosopher Aristotle's quotation about term limits must have seemed shocking to many who had lived under monarchs and religious leaders who ruled for life:

> But that judges of important causes should hold office for life is not
> a good thing, for the mind grows old as well as the body.
> —Aristotle, *The Politics*, 320 BCE

Loyalty to Old World monarchs might have lasted a lot longer in the future American colonies if Europeans had not learned about democracy after the mid-1400s. Newly educated Europeans began to ask questions about government. Where did it come from? What was the purpose of it? What rights did a government owe its people? What did the people owe rulers?

Radical questions about government spread throughout Europe on the eve of the **Age of Exploration**. They challenged royal and church leaders of Christopher Columbus's time. Those who benefitted from the old ways of ruling fought change. European kings, queens, church leaders, and members of the aristocracy held on to their authority with all their might. Yet not one boarded the ships for the dangerous voyages to the New World after 1492.

However, risk-taking explorers, investors, and colonists did. European settlers put thousands of miles of ocean between themselves and their homelands. Some brought their home governments with them. Others left them behind.

The marriage of King Ferdinand of Aragon and Queen Isabella of Castile united two kingdoms into the Spanish nation.

FERDINAND AND ISABELLA TIGHTEN THEIR RULE

Christopher Columbus benefited from good timing. He presented his Asian exploration plan to King Ferdinand and Queen Isabella (1479–1516) of Spain at the very time that the monarchs were ready to sponsor voyages to the East. As the world would later discover, Columbus did not reach China or India, which Europeans called the Indies. Instead, he found riches in the Western Hemisphere—an area that had been all but unknown in Europe.

Upon Columbus's return, Ferdinand and Isabella made plans for future voyages. They also moved quickly to reorganize their monarchy to ensure there would be no democracy that Europeans were beginning to read about. The king and queen limited the powers of feudal lords in Spain. They put financial, military, and legal institutions directly under their control. Their highly structured royal government would make it as clear as possible to their subjects that the king and queen held absolute power. That included the Spanish colonists who would settle in the New World. Just as commoners in Spain could not participate in government, neither would Spanish colonists.

At the same time, Ferdinand and Isabella formed a partnership with Pope Alexander VI, who granted Spain the exclusive right to explore and claim any lands beyond a north-south line drawn 320 miles (515 kilometers) to the west of the Cape Verde Islands (Portugal was given the land east of that boundary). With this move, the king and queen believed they had expanded their control of everyone living on Spanish-occupied land.

Ferdinand and Isabella sponsored twelve more voyages to the New World—but they would discover that it was easier to rule their nearby subjects with an iron hand than their colonists across the Atlantic. Stirrings of independence began almost as soon as explorers and colonists set foot on western shores.

THE FRENCH KINGS REINFORCE POWER

King Louis XI (1461–1483) spent France's precolonial period strengthening his monarchy. He reorganized the government, the military, and the law and put them under direct royal control. As in Spain, the monarchy also strength-

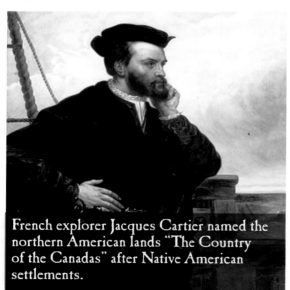

French explorer Jacques Cartier named the northern American lands "The Country of the Canadas" after Native American settlements.

ened its partnership with the Catholic clergy in France. This increased the king's power and that of the monarchs who would succeed him.

When King Louis XIV (1643–1715) came to the throne, the French monarchy was as powerful as it had ever been. To compete with Spain, the king decided to extend France's power around the world. In the 1500s, France sponsored the explorers Giovanni da Verrazano, Jacques Cartier, and Samuel de Champlain. They claimed land in the West Indies and in North America for France. These included areas in the Mississippi River valley, Canada, and the Carolinas, just north of Spanish-controlled Florida.

GOING FOR GOLD

The economic theory called mercantilism, which was used in Europe in the seventeenth and eighteenth centuries, had a major effect on the colonies in North America. This theory promoted the government regulation of its country's economy in order to increase state power at the expense of one's rivals. One of the primary ideas of mercantilism was that acquiring of gold was necessary for a strong state, and that to build gold reserves a nation had to have a very favorable trade balance. This meant that the nation had to export many more goods than it imported.

One way to guarantee favorable trade balances was to start colonies to provide raw materials to the homeland that could be made into goods for export. The colonies were prevented from manufacturing and from trading with anyone except the founding countries. This created trade **monopolies** and hampered the growth of the colonies.

Eventually, the French lost most of their American colonies. Unlike the Spanish king and queen, King Louis XIV had "outsourced" colonization to private businesses. The French king gave **charters** to private business groups, creating monopolies. They were to develop colonies at their own expense. They were to send goods back to the Old World and could only buy goods from France.

King Louis XIV, however, feared the independence and power of the monopolies after colonization was under way. He shortened the charters or cancelled them altogether to gain more control over New World riches. Without full royal support, along with wars against England and Native Americans, the private French mercantile groups failed at large-scale colonization. Wars with the English and with Native Americans eventually ended French colonization south of Canada.

The Dutch Business Model

During the Age of Exploration, the Netherlands was a collection of seven smaller state-like provinces. Each had its own local government, not a single king or queen as in Spain, France, or England. When these smaller Dutch provinces had common interests such as defense or trade, they united in a larger, single government. That made the Dutch government of the 1500s a **republic**. Power moved up from individual landowners who chose leaders, not down from a king or queen. In 1648, this unified republic had, in fact, declared its independence from Spain, which had ruled the Netherlands for over two hundred years.

> "A man cannot govern a nation if he cannot govern a city; he cannot govern a city if he cannot govern a family; he cannot govern a family unless he can govern himself; and he cannot govern himself unless his passions are subject to **reason**" Dutchman Hugo Grotius, 1625

As a republic, each of the seven Dutch provinces sent government representatives to an **assembly**. If this kind of government organization sounds familiar, it is because some of the men who composed the United States Constitution knew about it. In the 1700s, they would organize the Atlantic colonies similar to the way the Dutch had organized their provinces. The result would change the multiple colonies in the Atlantic region into one United States.

The New Netherlands Colony lasted just sixty-two years. Company directors required its colonial farmers to work for the company as renters, not owners. This was not the kind of democratic republic Dutch colonists knew from back home. Few Dutch were willing to settle in a strange land where they would have less say in government than they enjoyed in the prosperous Netherlands. Weak immigration into the New Netherlands, along with ongoing wars with England, led to the failure of Dutch colonization in the New World after 1664. England easily took over New Netherlands, which the English renamed New York.

All the same, several features of the Old World Dutch government left an imprint. First, the Netherlands government made up of small provincial states was a living example of representative rule. Second, when those provinces had united into one government, they had successfully declared their independence from Spain. From this event, rebellious American colonists of the 1700s learned that a unified government made up of small states could overthrow a superpower.

Dutchman Hugo Grotius wrote the most important international laws governing the seas in 1609.

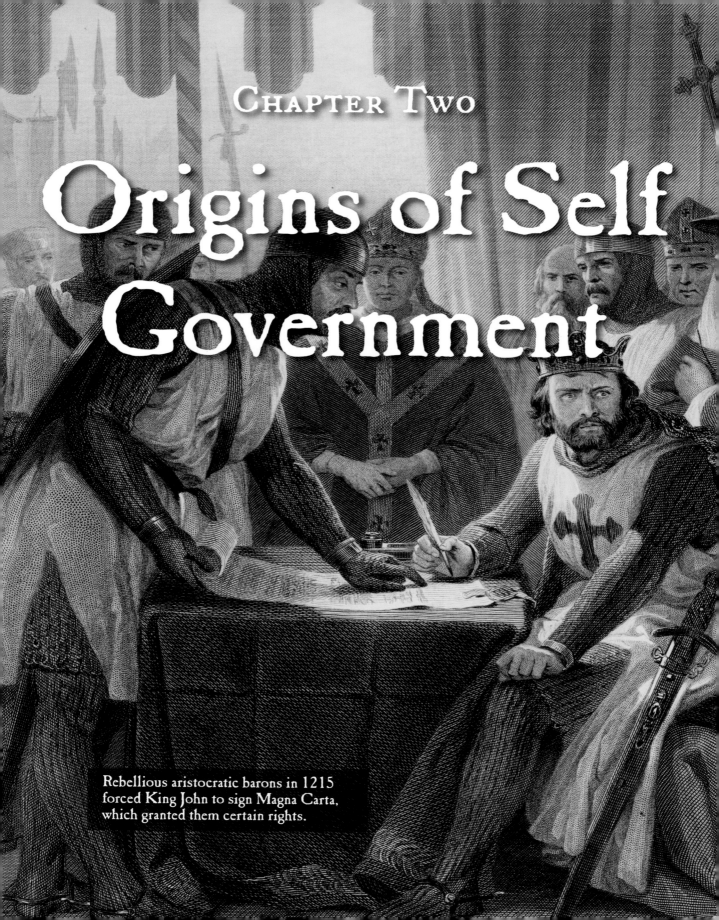

Chapter Two

Origins of Self Government

Rebellious aristocratic barons in 1215 forced King John to sign Magna Carta, which granted them certain rights.

No Freeman shall be taken or imprisoned, or be disseised of
[separated from] his Freehold [property], or Liberties, or free
Customs, or be outlawed, or exiled, or any other wise destroyed;
nor will We not pass upon him, nor condemn him, but by lawful
judgment of his **Peers**, or by the Law of the Land. (1)
—**Magna Carta**, 1215

No one in England was thinking about future American colonies in 1215. That is when an organized group of rebellious aristocrats forced King John to sign away some of his absolute power and give it to the lords who served him. This demand for rights from a monarch was previously unheard of in European countries. The document the English lords forced the king to sign was the Magna Carta. The restriction placed limitations on the absolute rule of present and future English monarchs.

Not even a king could take away a lord's land or freedom. No lord accused of a crime could be punished or executed without the judgment of his peers. Like his aristocratic subjects, the king had to observe the law of the land. These were a collection of **English common laws** that judges used for hundreds of years. Many of these laws would form the foundation of American laws.

The rights outlined in the Magna Carta applied only to "freemen"—males who owned large and small estates. Though the Magna Carta gave new rights to just five percent of the English population, the remaining ninety-five percent received their first look at democracy. While it did not yet apply to them, they did realize that even the king had to share power. Four hundred years into the future, English colonists would organize a democratic government. The centerpiece of that American government would be the Magna Carta.

The English upper classes did not stop their demands for rights with the Magna Carta. Educated citizens learned about the benefits of shared power from reprinted ancient texts. The philosopher Aristotle thought that the ideal government was an organization of representatives in which the monarch, the aristocracy, and ordinary citizens shared power. "The constitution is better which is made up of more numerous elements," he wrote.

Such thinking among English aristocrats led to the passage of the **Petition of Right** in 1628. This gave lords and gentry the right to serve as elected representatives in a governing body called **Parliament**. Property-owning freemen could no longer be forced to open their homes to soldiers. A king or queen could not go to war or raise taxes without Parliament's permission.

The experience of new freedoms and rights was unstoppable. In 1689, Parliament passed the **English Bill of Rights**. Property-owning citizens now had the right to vote in free elections. Prisoners could not be charged with excessive bail or punished with cruel methods. A king or queen could not interfere with a person's freedom of speech. Nor could he or she suspend any common laws without Parliament's permission. The Founding Fathers of the United States would promote these same rights.

> Freedom of religion, freedom of the press, trial by **jury**, habeas corpus [bringing an accused person to trial], and a representative **legislature** ... I consider as the essentials constituting free government.
> —Thomas Jefferson, 1815

What Were They Thinking?

As books and education spread throughout Europe in the 1600s and 1700s, so did debates about government. Some scholars challenged the established order by stating that government first arose from the needs of society, not from a divine or supreme figure. Therefore, government should be organized with a constitution planned by the people, not by absolute rulers like kings, queens, or church authorities. Leaders were to fulfill the rights and needs of the people, and not the other way around.

Several important philosophers thought that every individual was born with reason, a logical, orderly way of thinking and problem solving. "Reason is natural revelation," the English scholar John Locke (1632–1704) argued in the "Politics of Moral Consensus." He wrote that a person's labor was a kind of personal "property" that no one else could take away. The purpose of government was to preserve this earned, rightful property.

The movement that emphasized individual reason, property, and freedom came to be called the **Enlightenment**. Thinkers in the movement suggested practical ways to organize government. A number of them said government authority needed to be shared in a system of **checks and balances** and **separation of powers**.

Among these surprisingly, was a French nobleman, Charles-Louis de Secondat, Baron de La Brède et de Montesquieu. In 1752, he wrote in *The Spirit of Laws*, Volume I, "Again, there is no liberty, if the judiciary power be not separated from the legislative and executive … There would be an end of everything, were the same man or the same body, whether of the nobles or of the people, to exercise those three powers, that of enacting laws, that of executing the public resolutions, and of trying the causes of individuals."

Others declared that no leader—not even a king or a queen—was born with the right to command others. This countered the concept of Divine Right, which stated that monarchs gained their legitimacy, which could not be taken from them, through ancestors who had been appointed by God. Rulers had formulated this concept to consolidate their power and to fend off any claims of authority by the Pope in temporal or spiritual matters. In the new view, leaders had to answer to individuals who had the power of reason to govern themselves.

WORDS OF CHANGE

John Locke on Reason

    Reason, which is that Law that teaches all Mankind, who would but consult it, that being all equal and independent, no one ought to harm another in his Life, Health, Liberty, or Possessions ...

Denis Diderot on Leaders

    No man has received from nature the right to command his fellow human beings.

Jean Jacques Rousseau on Freedom

Every man having been born free and master of himself, no one else may under any pretext whatever subject him without his consent. To assert that the son of a slave is born a slave is to assert that he is not born a man.

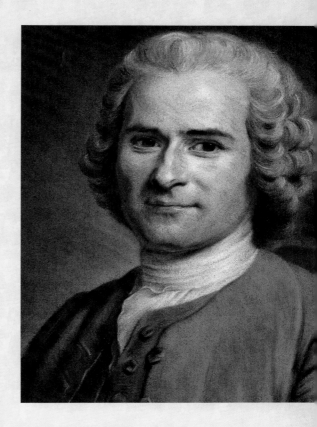

John Milton on Freedom of Speech

Give me the liberty to know, to utter, and to argue freely according to conscience, above all liberties.

CHAPTER THREE

Government by Charter

Christopher Columbus agrees to the terms
of the charter King Ferdinand and Queen
Isabella granted him.

Our will is, That you, Christopher Columbus, after discovering
and conquering the said Islands and Continent in the said ocean, or
any of them, shall be our Admiral of the said Islands and Continent
you shall so discover and conquer; and that you be our Admiral,
Vice-Roy, and Governour in them and that for the future, you may
freely ... decide all causes, civil and criminal ... as you shall think fit
in justice, and as the Admirals of our kingdoms use to do; and that
you have power to punish offenders ...
—Privileges and Prerogatives Granted by Their Catholic Majesties
to Christopher Columbus, 1492

Explorers who left the Old World from 1492 onward did not arrive on America's shores with England's Magna Carta in one hand and the Petition of Right in the other. The goal of New World explorations was profit, not democracy. Therefore, the European monarchies—and the Dutch government—that sponsored the New World voyages handed over contracts and charters to men adventurous enough to explore unknown lands.

Charters were the New World's start-up constitutions. They spelled out just how explorers and later settlers were to colonize and govern any foreign lands they found. To encourage colonists to settle in the New World, some charters granted them more freedoms than citizens had back home. Overall, monarchs and business **sponsors** expected the explorers to transplant the governments of the mother country into the conquered lands.

The contract and privileges King Ferdinand and Queen Isabella granted to Christopher Columbus, who was Italian, were the same titles and governing powers royal aristocrats possessed in Spain.

The king and queen of Spain did not foresee that transplanting the Spanish government in a land thousands of miles away would be easier said than done. Conditions in the New World led Columbus, and the Spanish conquistadors who followed, to make independent decisions at odds with their charters. Some secretly enriched themselves. Some committed crimes against Native Americans. Some had children outside marriage with Native women.

Once colonization was under way, the monarchs learned that the conquistadors were violating their charters. The king and queen stripped Columbus and other conquistadors of their government titles and authority. They sent their own handpicked colonial representatives to enforce Spanish law in the New World. The crown and the church, not the conquistadors, would try to recreate a Spanish government in its New World colonies.

THE LONG SHADOW OF THE ENGLISH KING

King James's 1606 English charter to the Virginia Company (and a similar one for the Plymouth Colony after they set up their own colony) began with a high-minded goal. Colonists were to bring Christianity to any lands that England conquered:

> Wee, greatly commending and graciously accepting of theire desires to the
> furtherance of soe noble a worke which may, by the providence of Almightie
> God, hereafter tende to the glorie of His Divine Majestie in propagating of
> Christian religion to suche people ...
> —The First Virginia Charter, 1606

These instructions about bringing Christianity to the New World consisted of a hundred words or so. England sent over a few members of the clergy to bring faith to the New World.

However, King James devoted thousands more words to the founding of English colonies for profit. The king's charter to the Virginia Company told its leaders to organize a government council of thirteen business merchants. The king named a second council in England to supervise business matters con-

ALL BUSINESS FOR NEW NETHERLANDS

By the mid-1500s, the Netherlands had grown rich from its Asian and Caribbean colonies. Dutch leaders had learned that a controlling company form of government was the way to riches. The business leaders who enjoyed a form of democracy in the Netherlands did not extend such freedom to their North American colonists. The Dutch West Indies Company charter focused on governing the North American colony to gain maximum profit.

> ... there shall be erected one General Company. That, moreover, the aforesaid Company may, in our name and authority, within the limits herein before prescribed ... make contracts, engagements and alliances with the princes and natives of the countries comprehended therein, and also build any forts and fortifications there, to appoint and discharge Governors, people for war, and officers of justice, and other public officers, for the preservation of the places, keeping good order, police and justice, and in like manner for the promoting of trade ...

—Charter of the Dutch West India Company, 1621

Dutch leaders saw New Netherlands through the eyes of profit-seeking businessmen. The Dutch West India Company's rigid form of government had the opposite effect of what leaders back home had hoped for: it discouraged colonization. Fewer Dutch colonists made the trip across the Atlantic than colonists from other countries. Why should they give up the freedoms they enjoyed in the Netherlands for less freedom in New Netherlands?

THE
GENERALL HISTORIE
OF
Virginia, New-England, and the Summer
Isles: with the names of the Adventurers,
Planters, and Governours from their
first beginning An: 1584. to this
present 1624.

With the Proceedings of those Severall Colonies
and the Accidents that befell them in all their
Journyes and Discoveries.

Also the Maps and Descriptions of all those
Countryes, their Commodities, people,
Government, Customes, and Religion
yet knowne.

DIVIDED INTO SIXE BOOKES.

By Captaine IOHN SMITH sometymes Governour
in those Countryes & Admirall
of New England.

LONDON.
Printed by I.D. and
I.H. for Michael
Sparkes.
1624.

The 1624 diaries of colonist Captain John Smith were later published in England.

cerning the colonies. The king authorized the Virginia Company councils to search for gold, silver, and copper wherever they could. Part of any riches they found would belong to the monarch and his successors.

Unlike early Spanish and Dutch colonists, English colonists had some say in choosing their council representatives. All the same, the English king's charters made clear that colonists worked for the monarch-approved Virginia Company, not strictly for themselves. A portion of the profits would go back to England and the crown. Colonists were forbidden to trade independently with foreign colonies or countries.

King James's charter reflected the Old World power structure. The English monarchy had the ultimate power over the colonies and the colonists. Still, the first English settlers who came to America had already experienced some independent rights under Magna Carta, the Petition of Right, and an elected Parliament. They were not about to give them up just because they were thousands of miles away. By the late 1600s, English colonists would begin to demand the same rights on their side of the Atlantic.

CHAPTER FOUR

Colonists Start to Pull Away

The leading male passengers on the Mayflower created their own government document while at sea in 1620.

*... And well knowing where a people are gathered together the word of God requires that to maintain the peace and union of such a people there should be an orderly and decent Government established according to God, to order and dispose of the affrays of the people at all seasons as occasion shall require; do therefore associate and connive ourselves to be as one Public State or **Commonwealth** ...*
—The Fundamental Orders, 1639

The first stirrings of colonial independence from a sponsoring country began during an accident of geography: like Christopher Columbus, a ship's captain got lost. Christopher Jones's ship, the *Mayflower*, had left England in the fall of 1620 after a series of delays. Its destination was the Virginia Colony. There, a handful of farmers and **indentured servants** hoped to build new lives, along with a large group of Pilgrims escaping poverty and religious harassment in England and on the continent. As the leader of the Pilgrims, William Bradford said, "… the place they had thoughts on was some of those vast and unpeopled countries of America, which are fruitful and fit for habitation." Instead of reaching the Virginia Colony, however, the *Mayflower* landed on the shores of what is now Cape Cod.

After their disastrous journey, during which several passengers died and many fought and bickered, the travelers found themselves in a kind of no-man's land. They were not going to the Virginia Colony. They realized, therefore, that its charter did not bind them. That left them without a colony, a charter, or any official government permission to colonize at all. They could "use their own liberty; for none had power to command them …" To deal with their predicament, self-appointed leaders on the *Mayflower* created their own charter. Such a document would unite the passengers and help them participate in decisions about where to settle and how to govern themselves.

THE MAYFLOWER COMPACT OF 1620

We whose names are underwritten, the loyal subjects of our dread Sovereign Lord King James, by the Grace of God of Great England, France, and Ireland King, Defender of the Faith, etc.

Having undertaken, for the Glory of God and advancement of the Christian Faith and Honour of our King and Country, a Voyage to plant the First Colony in the Northern Parts of Virginia, do by these presents solemnly and mutually in the presence of God and one of another, Covenant and Combine ourselves together into a Civil Body Politic, for our better ordering and preservation and furtherance of the ends aforesaid; and by virtue hereof to enact, constitute and frame such just and equal Laws, Ordinances, Acts, Constitutions and Offices, from time to time, as shall be thought most meet and convenient for the general good of the Colony, unto which we promise all due submission and obedience. In witness whereof we have hereunder subscribed our names at Cape Cod, the 11th of November, in the year of the reign of our Sovereign Lord King James, of England, France and Ireland the eighteenth, and of Scotland the fifty-fourth. Anno Domini 1620.

The *Mayflower's* leaders also understood the unexpected advantage of their situation. Without the official authority of the Virginia Colony, *Mayflower* passengers could organize their own colony and place it under a charter to their own liking. The new charter was called the Mayflower Compact.

With the signatures of most of the adult male passengers, the Mayflower Compact was a declaration of some independence from England. While the Compact promised obedience to God and the king, the signers also gave themselves the right to establish the new Plymouth Colony. The Mayflower Compact recognized King James of England, but it did not bear his wax seal or signature. The signatures of *Mayflower* passengers were all that counted.

THE PRE-CONSTITUTION CONSTITUTION

The religious Pilgrims and Congregationalists in what was to become the Connecticut Colony were fed up. Since 1630 or so—even before the colony was formed in 1636—they had been asking the Anglican Church for reforms. The changes the colonists wanted from England took so long that the disgruntled leaders took matters into their own hands. In 1639, they created the Fundamental Orders under the leadership of Roger Ludlow. This document spelled out the Connecticut Colony's rules for self-government, without England's permission. Except for Ludlow, the men—landowners, ministers, and **magistrates**—did not sign the document for fear of punishment from England. However, they did follow the Orders.

Authors of the Fundamental Orders supposedly hid their document from English officials in this Hartford, Connecticut, oak tree, which fell in a windstorm in 1856.

The Fundamental Orders described the rights that free men had. The document also outlined government limits, so that it could not overpower individuals. Property-owning free men gave themselves the right to vote by a secret paper ballot. (This right was not given to women, indentured servants, or slaves, however.) These rights were "firsts" in the English colonies. Many of them reappeared over a hundred years later in the United States Constitution.

England, under King Charles II, replaced the Fundamental Orders with yet another royal charter in 1662. Since England needed its colonies, the king's charter did allow the colonists to keep some of the freedoms in the Fundamental Orders.

When King James II came to power, he integrated the Northeastern colonies and New York back into one New England colony—thereby consolidating control—and asked Connecticut to surrender the 1662 Charter. In 1687, the charter was placed on a table between a party led by Sir Edmond Andros, representing the crown, and Connecticut governor, Robert Treat, and the issue was debated. In the evening, candles somehow were extinguished. The charter disappeared in the darkness.

Legend has it the charter was passed through a window and hidden in a large tree called the Charter Oak. Regardless, it was never surrendered. The reign of James II was short, and in 1692 the new rulers of England, William and Mary, were convinced to confirm the 1662 charter.

The legendary tree fell in a windstorm in 1856.

Smugglers, Tax Dodgers, and Lawbreakers

Documents such as the Mayflower Compact and the Fundamental Orders were not the only ways colonists declared some independence from home countries. Many found their way around restrictive laws they did not like. Spanish ranchers ignored some of the Laws of the Indies, which forbade settlers from forcing Native Americans to work for them. Many French fur trappers hunted where they wished and traded with whomever they wished without always reporting their profits to the crown back in France.

New England and Middle Atlantic colonists were furious about England's Navigation Acts in 1651. These laws restricted colonial traders from importing or exporting goods with countries other than England. The Molasses Act, for example, forced English colonists to buy the syrup from the English West Indies only.

Colonists grew increasingly rebellious as England imposed more laws and more taxes on its American holdings.

Colonists did more than protest. They acted. They knew that the home country rulers were thousands of miles away. England, France, and Spain could hardly afford to send enough officials or tax collectors to control trade. Even if there were enough officials to enforce the laws, local magistrates were often on the side of the lawbreakers.

Smuggling, tax avoidance, and bending the laws became socially acceptable ways for colonists to protest unfair regulations. The English accused ship owner John Hancock, one of the signers of the Declaration of Independence, of smuggling. Another signer, John Adams, helped to get Hancock's smuggling charges dropped. Many of the most respectable shippers bribed English tax officials to look the other way when foreign goods found their way onto colonial ships. Smuggling and breaking inconvenient laws changed the relationships between colonists and the home government. "Gateway" protests paved the way for more direct protests, such as the Stamp Act Protest and Boston Tea Party, from the mid-1700s and beyond.

CHAPTER FIVE

Four Hundred Years of Spanish Government

Spanish Mission San José de Tumacácori can be visited today at the Tumacácori National Historical Park in Southern Arizona.

> ... the most beneficial thing that could be done at present would
> be to remove the said chiefs and Indians to the vicinity of the
> villages and communities of the Spaniards—this for many consid-
> erations—and thus, by continual association with them, as well as
> by attendance at church on feast days to hear Mass and the divine
> offices, and by observing the conduct of the Spaniards ... it is clear
> that they will the sooner learn them and, having learned them, will
> not forget them as they do now.
>
> —The Laws of Burgos, 1512

Spain had a head start in colonizing the New World after Columbus returned in 1493. Before other European countries could organize men and ships, Spain sent more explorers across the Atlantic Ocean. Conquistadors like Juan Ponce de León, Francisco Pizzaro, and Hernán Cortéz claimed vast territories on both continents of the Americas. Spain took over islands in the Caribbean, which had ideal growing conditions for sugar cane. It conquered territories in South and Central America, which were rich in silver and copper. To protect those interests, the conquistadors headed north from Mexico. They created a frontier by colonizing the **Spanish Borderlands** in North America. Along this border, Spain established colonial settlements in what are now Texas, Arizona, New Mexico, and California.

Spanish soldiers easily overwhelmed Native American bands and took over their hunting territories and villages. Native governments—tribes, chiefdoms, and confederacies that had existed for thousands of years—collapsed. The Native Americans could not defend themselves against Spanish soldiers who possessed what they did not—metal weapons, horses, and immunities to deadly diseases that killed millions. With the breakdown of Native American societies, Spaniards as well as Hispanics from the South American colonies tried to colonize great stretches of the Americas with their own settlers and government.

King Ferdinand and Queen Isabella had ordered the conquistadors and officials to govern the American colonies with the same laws and titles as their monarchy in Spain. They would have no Enlightenment ideas, no Mayflower Compact, no separation of powers, and no religious diversity in the Spanish colonies. Catholicism would be the only recognized religion.

After the conquistadors' initial colonization, the monarchs ended their contracts or shortened their terms. They created the Council of the Indies in 1524 to replace the conquistador governors with high-ranking government administrators. These **viceroys** traveled to Spain's New World colonies to rule large provincial territories. The Spanish Borderlands was one of them.

The crown closely supervised the viceroys, despite the great distance between Spain and the Americas. No detail was too small for the monarchy

Impressive cathedrals and churches, such as the Metropolitan Cathedral of the Assumption of Mary in Mexico City, were at the center of Spain's colonial settlements and cities.

GOVERNMENT IN COLONIAL AMERICA

to review. The viceroys needed permission for almost anything they wanted to do. The crown kept the viceroys' terms of office short. This was a way to prevent them from gathering too much power or wealth in the colonies, as the conquistadors had. Monarchs throughout the Spanish colonial period sent over inspectors to keep tabs on the viceroys. Documents and requests travelled back and forth on Spanish voyages. This heavy-handed government rule from afar would eventually weaken the Spanish Borderlands. Colonial leaders could not respond to issues as quickly or efficiently as leaders in other colonies later did.

REPARTIMIENTO AND ENCOMIENDA

Spain gained experience with colonial rule when it successfully colonized the Canary Islands off the coast of Africa in the 1400s. Once Spain had conquered the islands, the monarchy gave favored associates large, limited land grants called *repartimiento*, meaning "distribution." The owners of the grants soon turned the land into sugar plantations, where the Native population was forced to work.

The Spanish monarchs hoped to install the Canary Islands repartimiento land grant system in the Americas. The first grants went to conquistadors, military officers, and church officials in the Caribbean islands and South America. However, in the Americas, the monarchy needed an acceptable way to convert the conquered Native Americans to Catholicism while providing all the labor on its repartimiento lands without enslavement.

To accomplish these goals, the Spanish government installed a ruling system called the *encomienda*, which means "to entrust." Native Americans were entrusted to the repartimiento landowners in the southern Americas. They became responsible for converting and educating other Native Americans who lived on their land. In exchange for living on repartimiento lands, the Native Americans had to give tribute to their new masters in the form of labor, crops, minerals, and animals that came from the land.

The encomienda system in South America and the Caribbean islands cast aside existing Native American territories, religions, and governments. It forced

Some Spanish colonial landowners used forced labor in the encomienda system.

the Native Americans to work under brutal conditions. Many Spanish landowners used Native Americans as near slaves who had little voice or independence. For their labors, the Native American workforce got just enough to eat so that they could work. Profits went to the landowners. The Catholic Church would later pressure the monarchy to find alternatives to the repartimiento and encomienda systems in the Spanish Borderlands in North America.

The encomienda system eventually sickened and killed so many Native Americans that authorities in the home country grew alarmed. Spain needed the Native American labor force to develop its colonies. Church and government authorities attempted to control the encomienda system from afar. The monarchy issued the 1512 Laws of Burgos. The Laws called for more humane treatment of the Native Americans living on encomienda lands. Yet the first step, once again, was to dissolve the Native American governments. Catholic officials decided to relocate the Native people into villages that would be governed by Spaniards as well as by Catholic priests and **friars**.

The encomienda form of government rule in the Spanish Borderlands lasted until the mid-1500s. Landowners fought changes to their profitable arrangement, which depended on forced labor. Spain was too far away to dismantle the system right away. All the same, the Laws of Burgos paved the way for different kinds of colonial settlement and government.

MISSION GOVERNMENT

The movement of French and English soldiers through the Great Plains threatened the Spanish Borderlands. French and English soldiers had formed alliances with Native American bands of the Great Plains. They had armed some Native people and had given them horses. To keep the foreigners and their Native guides away, Spain created a system of well-run outposts. In partnership with the Catholic Church, Spain developed nearly two hundred religious **mission** communities. Most of them were located near existing Native American settlements called *pueblos*. Through the mission system, Spanish colonists hoped to strengthen their numbers by bringing the pueblo Natives into Spanish settlements.

The missions were also a way to remove Native Americans from the encomienda ranches. Mission priests would convert the Native Americans to Catholicism and a Spanish way of life. Friar Bartolomé de las Casas led the cause. De las Casas had been an encomienda landowner himself. After seeing the brutality of the system firsthand, he gave up his land grant and became a friar. He said: "... the greatest evil which has caused the total destruction of those lands (Native American territories) is the encomienda as it now exists."

The Catholic Church believed that the way to save the souls of the Native Americans was not by brutality but by living a way of life centered on the church. Catholic priests and friars modeled their missions after small farming and ranching villages back in Spain. They established nearly two hundred missions in the Spanish Borderlands from the 1500s to the mid-1700s in Texas, New Mexico, and Arizona. (They would develop more missions in California in the late 1700s.) In their eagerness to convert Native Americans, church officials pressured them to move to the missions, sometimes forcibly. So many were herded into the missions, in fact, that more Native Americans than Spaniards lived inside or outside them. The Church planned to turn over the missions to the Native Americans who lived there, but that never took place.

Mission settlements seemed like a recipe for colonial success. Conflicts, however, arose between the mission priests in New Spain and the monarchy's viceroys, governors, and mayors. Tensions developed for two reasons. First, the mission friars began to exercise independence from the Spanish government in running the missions. Second, the missions allowed something the Spanish government did not: they permitted the Native Americans living in the missions to participate in mission government. Friars organized elections for governors and other officers made up of Native American candidates of their own choosing.

Such government participation did not sit well with wealthy landowners and officials outside the missions. They appealed to the Spanish monarchy to crack down on the missions. In 1683, the monarchy authorized Spanish governors to choose representatives to deal with the missions. The small amount of

The Texas Alamo, founded as a mission church, became the center of rebellion against Spanish rule in 1836.

government power mission Native Americans had enjoyed was now decreased by the presence of these representatives. Spain returned to ruling its colonies with a heavy hand.

PRESIDIO GOVERNMENT

In the early 1700s, England and France had their eyes on central Texas, which Spain had claimed for itself. Spain's religious missions needed military protection. Spain ordered the development of the *presidio* system of about two hundred military forts. Spanish soldiers, priests, and friars located most presidios near mission villages in the Spanish Borderlands.

Presidio San Antonio de Bexar was one of them. Its form of government was the same as that in military forts in Spain—military command. Located on the Rio Grande River, Presidio San Antonio de Bexar was founded in 1718. Four years later, the presidio was relocated to the other side of the river, a mile from an important mission.

Presidio San Antonio de Bexar was a rather plain structure. Its main building was made of hardened mud called adobe. It was topped with a grassy, thatched roof. Huts made of brush housed the soldiers. About two hundred soldiers and their families and a few settler families lived at Presidio San Antonio de Bexar. The presidio lacked protective walls or stockade fencing, so the Native Americans attacked it regularly. Still, the presidio did the job of staking Spain's claim to the area. Soldiers from Presidio San Antonio de Bexar protected five missions. It served as a communication center for people traveling through the area. It protected supply convoys from Mexico. It provided military escorts for New Spain's officials passing through. The city of San Antonio eventually grew around the fort. Presidio San Antonio de Bexar performed all its functions until Texas's gained its independence from Spain in 1836.

The Quarari Ruins from the Salinas Pueblo Mission in New Mexico are now a National Monument.

Town Government and Voting

While other countries' colonial towns and cities would arise to support a farming economy, Spanish colonial towns developed from the opposite direction. To attract immigrants, Spain specifically created municipal settlements first and parceled out surrounding farmland to support the towns. Spain allowed a minimal amount of government participation through a small town council called the *cabildo*, which was modeled on the same municipal government system back in Spain. Conquistadors who settled in towns quickly installed the cabildo system. This gave the conquistadors an institution to control local government.

A mayor, whom the provincial governor appointed, supervised the cabildo. Two magistrates served on the cabildo as a kind of combined police and judicial force to deal with criminals. A dozen or so elected male landowners filled the remaining council positions. Property owners had the right to elect their

Taxing problem

The one problem the cabildos could not address was the larger problem Spain had with the Spanish Borderlands—the lack of funds to support this frontier. They had yet to discover any natural resources or valuable minerals—such as the silver later found in Arizona and New Mexico—that would enable the territory to pay for itself, let alone make a profit. Colonists could only grow enough crops or raise enough livestock on the mostly dry, desert land to feed themselves and soldiers in the presidios. Yet Spain had to find some way to pay for its soldiers.

To solve the problem, the viceroys and governors placed taxes on tobacco, playing cards, some printed materials, and other items soldiers and colonists needed or wanted. Resentment of these taxes not only weakened the settlers' loyalty to the Spanish crown, it fueled their rebellion against their viceroy and other officials governing from Mexico City. All of the colonies in the Spanish Borderlands, except for Cuba and Puerto Rico, would be independent by the 1820s.

own representatives to serve on the cabildo. Women, indentured servants, and Native Americans living in the towns did not vote or participate in the cabildo councils.

The cabildo system mirrored city and town governments in Spain. The Spanish Borderlands, however, were thousands of miles away. Despite all their laws about how to design and administer towns, royal officials could not be on the ground in Spanish Borderland cities such as Santa Fe, New Mexico; Tuscon, Arizona; or Santa Barbara, California. It was in these municipal settlements where property-owning colonists experienced a taste of self-government. They needed to build local roads to move goods, crops, and livestock to and from the surrounding farming areas. They needed laws to control crime. They needed locals, not Mexico City viceroys or provincial governors, to settle local land and water disputes. The cabildo council addressed these problems.

Crime and Punishment

The Spanish Borderlands were wild lands, far from Spain. The first colonists were expected to apply complicated Spanish laws to local problems. Few lawyers were available to interpret Spanish laws. Therefore, local people took liberties in carrying out the laws. The views of the community were often more important than following Spain's strict legal codes to the letter.

Because the Spanish Borderlands had been conquered by force, violence was not uncommon in settling disputes. Almost a fifth of all crimes between 1700 and 1780 were murders. Assaults accounted for about third of the crimes committed in the Spanish Borderlands. Thefts, smuggling, cheating, drunkenness, and gambling made up the rest.

Imprisonment for violating even the worst of such crimes was not always the first step. So few colonists settled in the Spanish Borderlands, it made more sense for the colonies to reform criminals by putting them to work rather than locking them up. Public shaming was another way communities tried to control criminal behavior. A cattle thief might be forced to parade before his community with cattle intestines around his neck. Someone who assaulted a victim might be expected to make a public apology and take care of medical costs. Often, the town magistrates imposed fines on a criminal. Repeat offenders might be sent away. Still, the Spanish colonies needed labor more than they needed imprisoned, able-bodied criminals.

Such adaptations to Spanish government rules weakened the bonds between the colonists and their native country. In the end, heavy-handed rules, lack of financial support, and the growing demands for taxes broke the connection between Spain and its colonies. One province after another in New Spain declared its independence from the monarch-led home country. While Spain had had over a four-hundred-year run in the Americas, what began in 1492 ended in 1898 with the Spanish-American War.

CHAPTER SIX

The Government that Came to Stay

American colonists burn the dreaded tax stamps that English politicians attached to everyday goods the colonists needed.

The majority having, as has been shewed, upon men's first uniting into society, the whole power of the community naturally in them, may employ all that power in making laws for the community from time to time, and executing those laws by officers of their own appointing; and then the form of the government is a perfect democracy ...?

—John Locke, The Second Treatise of Civil Government, 1690

W hy did self-government take hold so quickly in England's American colonies, but not in those of Spain, France, and the Netherlands? After all, the governments of all four countries were fairly similar. Monarchs ruled in three of them—Spain, France, and England. (The Netherlands was the exception. Its home government was made up of provincial representatives.) All four sent explorers and colonists with charters for governing in the New World. The leaders of all four countries handpicked representatives to set up strong colonial governments. Yet the colonies that most influenced the founding of the United States were English. Self-government came to the English colonies for several reasons.

EMIGRATION

By encouraging undesirable groups to emigrate, England solved two problems. It populated its colonies and freed itself of people whom it regarded as social problems. These included religious nonconformists such as the Puritans, Pilgrims, and Quakers, the unemployed, the almost-unemployed lower middle class, the poor, and criminals. The religious protestors who emigrated were devout, family groups who quickly built up the population of the New England colonies. The downtrodden folk who were forced to leave England as indentured servants provided a workforce for Virginia and Carolina tobacco and rice plantations that became successful.

Spain, France, and the Netherlands had no such emigration plans for their North American colonies. They never attracted enough settlers to build strong colonies.

NOBLE EXPERIMENT

Englishman James Oglethorpe came up with a solution to the problem of jails crowded by people guilty of nothing more than being in debt. He was granted a charter in 1732 to found a colony for the "worthy poor" by King George II, and was appointed as one of the twenty-one trustees of the colony. The king backed the founding of Georgia primarily to create a land buffer between Spanish Florida and the Carolinas.

The trustees interviewed candidates to found the colony and selected skilled craftsmen and businessmen to ensure its success. Not one of the 114 men, women, or children selected had been in a debtors' prison, and few debtors ever settled there.

Georgia stands out for several reasons. It was the first colony established in fifty years. It was Anglican—two of its first religious leaders were Charles and John Wesley, who would later return to England and found the Methodist movement. Oglethorpe allowed members of many persecuted religions to settle there, although Catholics were banned. Finally, it was, at first, an anti-slavery colony.

Slaves from the Carolinas were used to build Savannah, Georgia's first city, but Oglethorpe and his successors kept slavery out of the colony until the trustees returned their charter and Georgia became a royal colony in 1752. That's when the plantation system and slavery entered Georgia.

This Endenture Witnesseth that the Nancy Hedon

Shadrach Hudson

of Sussex County State of Delaware Doth Put and bind her
by & with the Consent of Tilghman Taylor a Justice of the peace
Son Evan Morgan an apprentice to Alexandrew Fisher of
the County and State aforsaid to learn the farming business
and after the manor of an apprentice the said Evan
Morgan an apprentice Shall well and faithfully to serve
from the Day of the Date hereof fourteen years and one month
he being now Six Years & Eleven months old, all which time
the said apprentice the said Master shall well and faithfully
serve his secrets keep and lawfull Command obey, shall not
Do any hurt to said Master, or willfully suffer it to be Deen
by others without giving notice thereof, the goods of said Master the said
apprentice shall not Embezzle or them lend, to any at any unlawfull
Games, shall not frequent tavern, tipling, houses, or house of bad
fame, or Shall not Contract Matrimony in the term aforsaid
and shall not at any time absent himself from said master
Without his Consent but in all things behave and Demean
himself as a good and faithfull apprentice aught to Do during
the term aforsaid, And the said Master Doth hereby
Oblige himself to teach as cause to be taught, the art and
Mystery of the farming business which he now follows, to the
best of his skill knowlage and ability, and the said Master
Is to find the said apprentice in goods, and sufficient
Clothing boarding and lodging, for such an apprentice to have
And is to give the said apprentice one Years Schooling
and a Suite of Cloths then face, worth Twenty Dollars on
Twenty Dollars, in Witness whereof we have hereunto
set our hands and affixed our Seals the first Day of
february in the Year of our Lord Eighteen hundred and
Twenty Three — 1823

Signed Sealed & delivered
in the Presants of

William Fisher   Before name Shadrach
Mary J Hudson   Hudson was interlined
mark
Tilghman Taylor

Shadrach his + Hudson   {Seal}
mark
Nancy + Hudson   {Seal}

Evan Morgan, age six, became an indentured servant to a farmer for fourteen years,
according to this contract.

PROPRIETARY CHARTERS

England wanted the riches that New World colonization would bring. The country's economic problems made it difficult to fund its colonies, however. To afford their overseas adventures, England's monarchs gave more control to wealthy **proprietors** than did the monarchs of Spain or France. English charters allowed proprietors to appoint governors and other colonial officials of their choosing. This made it more difficult for the crown to control the proprietors who began to rule themselves early on. The crown later tried to impose more control over the proprietary colonies in the late 1600s by appointing its own government officials. However, by then it was too late. The proprietors and colonists had already had a taste of self-rule under their original charters. Colonial assemblies and colonial legislatures modeled on Parliament openly disobeyed royal governors, sometimes arrested them, or made their lives in the colonies miserable.

Due to political problems at home, the English monarchy could not effectively supervise its colonies. Without strict supervision, English colonists under the proprietors began to demand more government participation. Above all, colonists and proprietors alike came from the tradition of the Magna Carta, the Petition of Right, and a free press. France and Spain censored printed materials. England did not. Papers, pamphlets, and books with Enlightenment ideas about the government came over with the English colonists.

EVERYONE A LANDOWNER

England, as France and Spain, granted rights to a few to develop huge territories in North America. In Virginia and the Carolinas, a small number of planters owned all the land. However, indentured servants who supplied plantation labor received about a hundred acres of land after they worked off their five- to seven-year contracts. This made them property owners for the first time in their lives. The men could vote and serve in government. Spain,

France, and the Netherlands kept land grants, and the government power that went with them, in the hands of a few.

From the start, New England and mid-Atlantic colonists had received plots of land. As property owners, they demanded a full say in government, just as property owners in England had.

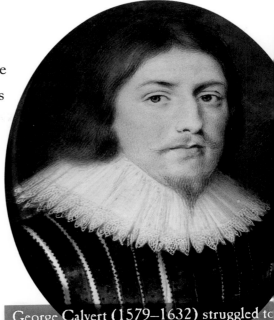

> Government being for the preservation of every
> man's right and property, by preserving him
> from the violence or injury of others, is for the
> good of the governed.
> —John Locke, First Treatise, 1689

Owning property and participating in government went hand in hand. The English colonies, more populated to begin with, had more property owners than rival colonial powers.

RELIGIOUS FREEDOM

Religious diversity was another reason English colonies prospered over those of other countries. Religious acceptance began in the English colonies in the late 1600s. Before that, religious groups such as the New England Pilgrims and Puritans confined themselves to their own colonies. They governed themselves as **theocracies**, keeping out anyone who practiced other religions—which was exactly what they had experienced in England. The Spanish and French colonies were Catholic.

As communications among the colonies improved, the religious colonies noted the benefits outsiders brought: population growth, new skills, and new ideas. Still, the colonies spent the early years of colonization trying to settle religious conflicts. Lord Baltimore, who founded Maryland as a refuge in the English colonies for Catholics, put into practice a law against religious intolerance to protect Catholic settlers.

The House of Burgesses in Virginia was America's first elected assembly.

> No person shall ... bee any waies troubled, Molested or discountenanced for or in respect of his or her religion nor in the free exercise thereof within this Province or the Islands thereunto belonging nor any way compelled to the beleife or exercise of any other Religion against his or her consent.
> —Lord Baltimore, Maryland Toleration Act, 1649

Lord Baltimore's Toleration Act was overturned and reinstated several times as Protestants and Catholics in Maryland continued to fight for religious control. Still, the Maryland Toleration Act introduced a major idea into England's colonies: no one's rights should be limited for religious reasons. This idea would eventually become part of the United States Constitution.

Pennsylvania thrived because William Penn welcomed everyone.

In time, other English colonial leaders put the practical needs of their colonies ahead of religious restrictions. They began to open their doors to immigrants of different religions and nationalities. The diverse skills and international connections immigrants brought to the English colonies boosted their economies over those of rival colonial powers.

The most successful of the English colonies in the 1700s was the Pennsylvania Colony. Its English leader, William Penn, was a Quaker. He believed the key to colonial success was a diverse population. To achieve this, he welcomed as many Quakers and non-Quakers as possible. He believed they all shared a single godliness.

> The humble, meek, merciful, just, pious and devout souls everywhere are
> of one religion and when death has taken off the mask, they will know one
> another, though the diverse liveries they wore here make them strangers.
> —William Penn, Fruits of Solitude, 1701

The Pennsylvania Colony attracted family-oriented, middle-class artisans, farmers, merchants, and traders who could not find religious havens elsewhere. The arrival of diverse, stable, talented people had the effect of linking tolerance with prosperity. The openness and success of the Pennsylvania Colony would become a model for more restrictive colonies over time.

> No people can be truly happy, though under the greatest enjoyments
> of civil liberties, if abridged of the Freedom of their Conscience as to
> their Religious Profession and Worship.
> —William Penn, Pennsylvania Charter of Liberties, 1701

CHAPTER SEVEN

By the People

The Charleston, South Carolina, harbor was the busiest trading port in the Southern colonies in the 1700s.

We ... by the authority of the good people of these colonies, solemnly publish and declare, that these united colonies are, and of
right ought to be free and independent states; that they are absolved
from all allegiance to the British Crown, and that all political connection between them and the state of Great Britain, is and ought to
be totally dissolved ...
—Declaration of Independence, July 4, 1776

At first, English colonies survived with little government. In the early 1600s, most colonists were farmers who did not require authoritative direction. They grew or hunted for their own food and harvested their own lumber for building. Most did not yet sell surplus crops, livestock, services, or goods that would require taxes and regulations for roads, ports, and warehouses.

Under the leadership of chartered proprietors who governed the settlers, early English colonial governments were sometimes shaky and disorganized. Distances between the colonies were so great, and travel so difficult, that each colony tended to go its own way. Colonists often knew more about what was going on in England than what was happening in other American colonies. That would soon change.

EXPANDING COLONIES, GOVERNMENT

Colonies that engaged in local and overseas trade began to expand their governments before more agricultural colonies did. In the mid-1700s, seaside and riverside ports developed into cities. Colonial cities began to need more government than rural areas did.

Urban dwellers and business owners needed to follow laws about property boundaries and behaviors that affected one another. Traders and merchants needed regulations to control weights and measures. Shippers needed government inspectors to check imported goods as well as tobacco, rice, lumber, and animal pelts for export. Colonial governments set prices that farmers, artisans, and shopkeepers could charge so that customers could trust businesses. Local

The work lives of Southern tobacco field slaves was much harsher than the lives of Northern slaves, who had more and safer work opportunities.

governments raised their own taxes to build docks and roads to ship or import goods. With townspeople living close together, property owners elected government officials to bring order to their towns. Town governments made laws to control crime, water use, building standards, and to fight fires.

Colonial governments became more formal in the 1700s. They mainly operated as top-down commonwealths. The faraway monarch and English Parliament ruled from the top. The colonial government, as well as church officials and the male heads of family households, had authority over everyone

SLAVE CODES

Each American colony had slaves after slave trading began between Barbados and Charles Town (now Charleston) in the Carolina Colony. The majority of slaves from Barbados went to work in the Chesapeake and southern "tobacco colonies"— Delaware, Maryland, Virginia, and the Carolinas. Colonial governments soon passed laws outlining rights and restrictions for masters and their slaves.

Slaves were considered an owner's property, so they had no right to property themselves. In most of the "tobacco and rice growing colonies," slaves were denied firearms, education, pay for work, marriage by choice, or the right to determine their children's future. They could not travel freely or grow food for themselves. Children of slave mothers were born as slaves. Slave labor was so important to the tobacco colonies that the punishment for runaway slaves was death. The northern colonial economies depended less on slave labor. Their governments' slave codes were less harsh than those in the plantation colonies. Slavery in the north resembled the indentured servant system in a few ways. Masters were allowed to set their slaves free.

Colonial governments required slave masters to uphold their colonies' slave codes or lose their slaves and pay a fine. Masters in the plantation colonies could not free their slaves or hide a runaway slave. Colonial government slave codes in the plantation colonies bound masters and slaves permanently.

below them. From top to bottom, everyone worked for the good of the community so that all could succeed in the commonwealth.

In the New England colonies, local government took place at **town meetings,** which met once a year to discuss town affairs. Anyone was allowed to speak at a town meeting, a custom still observed in New England. Male property owners voted for various male candidates to fill government positions in colonial legislatures. The wealthiest landowners headed up the government as well as church boards. Magistrates, **justices of the peace**, or constables handled criminal matters if the town-selected minister could not persuade a criminal to reform. Military officers and citizen militias kept themselves armed and ready to protect their communities. Town clerks managed taxation, which colonists wished to control locally, not from England. Loose pigs were rounded up and their careless owners were fined. Overseers planned and built highways, and went after anyone who blocked roads or bridges with carts, building materials, or fallen trees that owners had cut down on their properties. This was big government, colonial style.

In the Chesapeake and Southern colonies, wealthy plantation owners led a county system of government that covered large areas. Sheriffs or justices of the peace kept order over many miles. County magistrates ran the courts, licensed businesses, built roads, collected taxes, and enforced laws. Church and county government leaders were usually one and the same. They served on church boards, built churches, hired ministers, and helped the poor.

Governments in the plantation colonies of Delaware, Maryland, Virginia, and the Carolinas, which had regulated the indentured servant system, began to control the slave system as well. By the mid-1600s, English colonies began to import slaves to meet the growing need for labor on the plantations. Slaves first came from Africa to work on English colonial sugar plantations in Barbados and other Caribbean islands. From there, the practice of slavery moved to the plantations of the Southern colonies, then to all Eastern seaboard English colonies.

From Differences to Unity

The strict, religious Plymouth and the Massachusetts Bay colonies governed themselves under what they called Biblical law. The Quakers of Philadelphia adapted English laws that were more open than those of the mother country. The Chesapeake and Carolina colonies were rural, plantation based, and sparsely populated. Colonists who lived far apart in the countryside required a differ-

Patrick Henry riveted the Virginia House of Burgesses in 1775 with his cry: "Give me liberty, or give me death."

ent kind of government than village or townspeople in the northern colonies who lived closer together. A plantation economy required different regulations than a trading economy in a busy seaport. All of these separate needs prevented the English colonies from forming a common government.

Over a one hundred and fifty year period, however, the governments of England's separate colonies began to resemble one another. Due to trade among the colonies, easier travel, and the spread of printed materials, colonies shared their successful governing strategies.

What finally unified separate colonial governments, however, was the English monarchy. England reorganized its colonial administration to tighten its authority over trade in the early 1700s. It imposed new taxes on goods from the colonies and to the colonies. It restricted trade to English lands and English ships.

These heavy-handed changes energized all the American colonies. More royal control reminded them that they did not have the same full rights as English citizens across the Atlantic. They did not serve in the English Parliament, which constantly told them what to do. The English government had the right to tax them, judge them, regulate their economies, and review their laws. The colonies began to realize that developing their own legal institutions was a way of forging their independence.

It's the Law

Early colonists had arrived with some knowledge of English common laws and customs that had been in place for centuries. They brought law books from England to consult as they needed them. Trial by jury, indictments against an accused person, grand juries, and plea bargaining by admission of guilt, all had their roots in English legal traditions.

However, traditional English common laws and charters had their limits. Colonists found themselves in new situations that English laws did not always

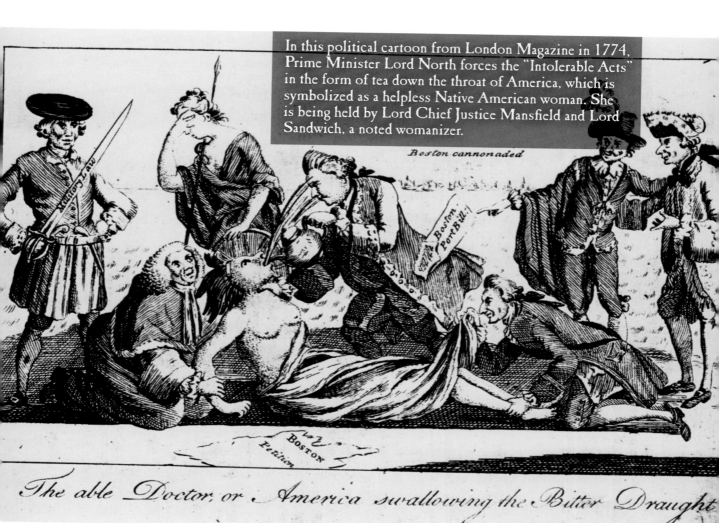

In this political cartoon from London Magazine in 1774, Prime Minister Lord North forces the "Intolerable Acts" in the form of tea down the throat of America, which is symbolized as a helpless Native American woman. She is being held by Lord Chief Justice Mansfield and Lord Sandwich, a noted womanizer.

The able Doctor, or America swallowing the Bitter Draught.

cover. They began to adapt traditional laws and create new ones to deal with conditions unique to the colonies. For example, the government of the Virginia House of Burgesses passed laws allowing most property owners to own guns. Back in England, most ordinary civilians could not carry guns—only soldiers were permitted to do so. American colonists needed their own firearms for protection from Native American and foreign attacks. They also needed fire-arms for hunting, an activity that was strictly regulated in England. The aristocracy there owned the forests and streams. With public, game-filled forests and countless rivers in colonial America, enforcing English common laws about hunting and fishing made no sense.

The Puritans of some New England colonies had their own ideas about government. Called by some "the Bible Commonwealths," these religious colonies created laws based on Bible teachings. The Old Testament of the Bible was often mentioned in New England's criminal laws.

In 1641, Massachusetts's colonists created the earliest colonial law code to protect many individual rights. This collection of civil laws was called the Body of Liberties: "… establishing of this government to collect and express all such freedoms as for present we foresee may concern us, and our posterity after us, and to ratify them with our solemn consent." These rights protected individuals from cruel and unusual punishment, from getting drafted into the military, from having property taken without payment or permission, and much more. They granted individuals everything from the right to a fair trial to the right to fish and hunt on public lands. The English government tried to restrict these new rights, but it did not succeed for long.

As they managed their own local governments and laws successfully, the colonies matured and felt connected to one another. Up and down the Atlantic seaboard, colonists began to form a proud American identity. When England took notice, it tried to impose tougher regulations, taxes, and laws than in the past.

By the time England imposed the Intolerable Acts, the colonies were ready to come together. The Continental Congress met for the first time in the fall of 1774. Twelve of the colonies sent representatives; only Georgia did not attend, as it was in need of the English soldiers. The twelve were divided on what course of action to take, and so rather than declare independence they sent a list of grievances to England and agreed to meet in 1775 if their concerns were not addressed.

The English Parliament ignored the grievances, and King George III condemned some of the colonists in a speech. This moved the Continental Congress to reconvene in Philadelphia on May 10, 1775.

After a long period of debate, the Declaration of Independence was unanimously approved on July 4, 1776. The Congress met throughout the Revolutionary War until it became the Congress of the Confederation, when the Articles of Confederation were ratified in 1781. These articles put most power in the hands of the states and gave the weak national government little power to force the states to act. Attendance by delegates dropped and Congress had difficulty gaining a quorum, so in 1787 a constitutional convention was called.

The convention's fifty-five delegates wrote a constitution heavily influenced by Enlightenment thoughts and ideas generated more than half a millennia earlier, and one that serves us today.

The 1776 Declaration of Independence cut the ties between the American colonists and the English government.

Glossary

absolute monarchs

Royal kings and queens who do not share power.

Age of Exploration

A period from 1400 to the 1700s when European explorers discovered lands previously unknown to them.

Americas, the

The combined land masses of North, Central, and South America.

aristocracy

An upper class connected to royalty which inherits its power and wealth through those connections.

assembly

A government group that passes laws and represents those who appoint or vote for them.

charters

Written rights and privileges a monarch gives a company, group, or an individual.

checks and balances

A system of government designed to maintain a balance of powers among several branches.

commoners

Middle- or lower-class ordinary people, usually without inherited power or wealth.

commonwealth

An independent community or a group of countries associated with a previous colonial power.

confederacy

An organization of self-governing groups that unite for a common cause.

constitution

A country's legal plan for organizing, regulating and running a government.

council

A group of appointed or elected government officials.

English Bill of Rights

A 1689 English document granting citizens the right to free elections as well as other rights.

English common laws

A collection of traditional laws by which English judges use previous rulings to decide the outcome of present cases.

Enlightenment

A way of thinking that began in the 1600s, which promoted an individual's reason and rights over traditional control by others.

friars

A community of religious men, such as the Franciscans or the Dominicans.

gentry

A class of male property owners of small areas of land.

governor

A colonial administrator or manager.

indentured servants

Workers obligated by contract to work for a certain time period, usually in exchange for receiving travel and daily expenses.

jury

Citizens who decide legal cases under the guidance of a judge.

justices of the peace

Magistrates appointed to hear minor cases, perform marriages, grant licenses, etc., in a town, county, or local district.

legislature

A group of elected representatives.

magistrates

A civil officer or lay judge who administers the law.

Magna Carta

The 1215 English document that limited a king's power and which strongly influenced the American Constitution.

mission

A settlement organized and run by a church.

monarchs

The royal leaders who inherit their positions or gain them militarily.

monopolies

Business privileges granting exclusive rights in territories or in markets.

New World

All the land in the Western Hemisphere.

Old World

African, Asian, and European lands in the Eastern Hemisphere.

Parliament

A branch of English government made up of the monarchy; the House of Lords, whose members have hereditary titles; and the House of Commons, to which representatives are elected.

peasant

A laborer who farms small parcels of land, which he may own or rent from others.

peers

People of equal standing or members of the English ruling class.

Petition of Right

A 1628 English document limiting many of the king's rights and granting citizens the right to participate in government.

proprietors

Individuals who have been granted the right to establish a colony.

reason

A logical way of thinking and making sense of the world based on observation.

republic

A government with elected representatives who appoint a leader.

separation of powers

A system of rule in which officials in different branches of government share power.

Spanish Borderlands

Spanish-controlled protective North American frontier regions, which included Texas, Arizona, New Mexico, and California.

sponsors

Supporters who funded explorers and businesses in the New World.

theocracies

Governments ruled by people of a single religion.

town meeting

A gathering of citizens who vote on a community's issues.

viceroys

The top officials representing a king or queen.

Further Reading

Books

Anderson, Dale. *Forming a New American Government*. New York, NY: Gareth Stevens Publishing, 2005.

Bain, David L., and Ann Leslie Tuttle. *Encyclopedia of the North American Colonies*. New York, NY: Charles Scribner's Sons, 1993.

Capaccio, George. *Life in Colonial America: Countryside*. New York, NY: Cavendish Square, 2014.

Colligan, L.H. *Life in Colonial America: The Cities*. New York, NY: Cavendish Square, 2014.

Cooke, Jacob Ernest, and Milton M. Klein, eds. *North America in Colonial Times*. New York, NY: Charles Scribner's Sons, 1998.

Dow, George Francis. *Every Day Life in the Massachusetts Bay Colony*. New York, NY: Dover Publications, 1988.

Hawke, David Freeman. *Everyday Life in Early America*. New York, NY: Harper & Row, 1988.

Rushforth, Brett, and Paul Mapp. *Colonial North America and the Atlantic World: A History in Documents*. New York, NY: Pearson Education, 2008.

Taylor, Alan. *The Settling of North America*, Volume I. New York, NY: Penguin Books, 2002.

Websites

American Colonies

www.digitalhistory.uh.edu

Collection of resources that provides short summaries and links to information about important topics in the history of the United States.

Government

americanhistory.about.com/od/colonialamerica/tp/
Colonial-Governments-Of-The-Thirteen-Colonies.htm

Capsule looks at each of the thirteen colonies that became the United States.

Original Documents

press-pubs.uchicago.edu/founders

Find primary source material in this collection of documents from our Founding Fathers.

Selected Bibliography

Andrews, Charles McLean. *American History: 1652-1689, Colonial Self Government*. Lecturable, 2012. (Kindle File)

Bain, David L. and Ann Leslie Tuttle. *Encyclopedia of the North American Colonies*. New York, NY: Charles Scribner's Sons, 1993.

Bolton, Herbert Eugene, *Spanish Borderlands*. Oklahoma: University of Oklahoma Press, 1964.

Bridenbaugh, Carl. *Cities in Revolt: Urban Life in America, 1743-1776*. New York, NY: Knopf, 1955.

Bridenbaugh, Carl. *Cities in the Wilderness: The First Century of Life in Urban America*, 1625–1742. New York, NY: Oxford University Press, 1971.

Cooke, Jacob Ernest, and Milton M. Klein, editors. *North America in Colonial Times, Volume 1*. New York, NY: Charles Scribner's Sons, 1998.

Cooke, Jacob Ernest, and Milton M. Klein, eds. *North America in Colonial Times, An Encyclopedia for Students*. New York, NY: Charles Scribner's Sons, 1998.

Diamond, Jared. *Guns, Germs, and Steel: The Fates of Human Societies*. New York, NY: W.W. Norton, 1999.

Dinkin, Robert J. *Voting in Provincial America: A Study of Elections in the Thirteen Colonies, 1689-1776*. Westport, CT: Praeger Publishers, 1977.

Jameson, J. Franklin, ed. *Narratives of New Netherland 1609-1664*. Charleston, SC: Bibliolife, 2009.

Mann, Charles. *1491: New Revelations of the Americas Before Columbus*. New York, NY: Knopf, 2005.

Osgood, Herbert L. *The American Colonies in the Eighteenth Century, Volume 1*. Gloucester, MA: Peter Smith Publishers, 1958. Retrieved March 7, 2014 from archive.org/stream/ americancolonies007864mbp#page/n5/mode/2up

Osgood, Herbert L. *The American Colonies in the Seventeenth Century, Volume 3*. London, England: The MacMillian Company, 1907. Retrieved March 7, 2014 from archive.org/stream/ 17thcenturycolonies03osgorich#page/n5/mode/2up

Rodriguez, Junius P., ed. *Slavery in the United States: A Social, Political, and Historical Encyclopedia, Volume 2*. Santa Barbara, CA: ABC-CLIO, Inc. 2007.

Rushforth, Brett and Paul Mapp. *Colonial North America and the Atlantic World: A History in Documents*. New York, NY: Pearson Education, 2008.

Taylor, Alan. *American Colonies*. New York, NY: Penguin Books, 2001.

Tyler, Lyon Gardiner, ed. *Narratives of Early Virginia, 1606-1625*. New York, NY: Charles Scribner's Sons, 1907.

Quotation Sources

Introduction: Spreading the Word

p. 5, Columbus, Christopher, "Letter to King Ferdinand of Spain, describing the results of the first voyage," retrieved March 19, 2014 from xroads.virginia.edu/~hyper/hns/garden/columbus.html

p. 7, Tyler, Lyon Gardiner, ed., *Narratives of Early Virginia, 1606–1625*, pp. 13–14.

Chapter 1: The Governments Back Home

p. 9, Aquinas, Thomas, *Summa Theologiae*, retrieved March 19, 2014 from cassian.memphis.edu/history/jmblythe/3370/ThomasAquinasGovernment.htm

p. 10, Polybius, *The Histories*, retrieved March 19, 2014 from thelatinlibrary.com/law/polybius.html

p. 10, Aristotle, *The Politics*, retrieved March 19, 2014 from www.constitution.org/ari/polit_02.htm

p. 14, Grotius, Hugo, *On the Law of War and Peace*, retrieved March 19, 2014 from thinkexist.com/quotation/a_man_cannot_govern_a_nation_if_he_cannot_govern/162070.html

Chapter 2: Origins of Self Government

p. 17, *Magna Carta*, retrieved March 19, 2014 from www.constitution.org/eng/magnacar.htm

p. 18, Aristotle, *The Politics*.

p. 18, Jefferson, Thomas, "Letter to Pierre Samuel du Pont de Nemours, 1815," retrieved March 19, 2014 from famguardian.org/Subjects/Politics/ThomasJefferson/jeff1770.htm

p. 19, Baron de Montesquieu, Charles de Secondat, *Spirit of Laws*, retrieved March 19, 2014 from www.constitution.org/cm/sol_11.htm

p. 20, Locke, John, *The Second Treatise on Civil Government*, retrieved March 19, 2014 from www.constitution.org/jl/2ndtr02.htm

p. 20, Diderot, Denis, *Encyclopédie*, retrieved March 19, 2014 from quod.lib.umich.edu/d/did/

p. 21, Rousseau, Jean Jacques, *Of The Social Contract, Or Principles of Political Right, Book IV*, retrieved March 19, 2014 from www.constitution.org/jjr/socon_04.htm

p. 21, Milton, John, *Areopagitica*, retrieved March 19, 2014 from, www.quotationspage.com/quote/29320.html

Chapter 3: Government by Charter

p. 23, "Privileges and Prerogatives Granted by Their Catholic Majesties to Christopher Columbus: 1492," retrieved March 19, 2014 from avalon.law.yale.edu/15th_century/colum.asp

p. 24, *The First Charter of Virginia, April 10, 1606*, retrieved March 19, 2014 from avalon.law.yale.edu/17th_century/va01.asp

p. 25, "Charter of the Dutch West India Company: 1621," retrieved March 19, 2014 from avalon.law.yale.edu/17th_century/westind.asp

Chapter 4: Colonists Start to Pull Away

p. 29, Bradford, William, *Of Plymouth Plantation*, retrieved March 19, 2014 from mith.umd.edu//eada/html/display.php?docs=bradford_history.xml

p. 30, Bradford, *Of Plymouth Plantation*.

p. 30, Bradford, *Of Plymouth Plantation*.

Chapter 5: Four Hundred Years of Spanish Government

p. 35, "1512-1513, The Laws of the Burgos," retrieved March 19, 2014 from faculty.smu.edu/bakewell/BAKEWELL/texts/burgoslaws.html

p. 40, Rodriguez, Junius P., ed., *Slavery in the United States: A Social, Political, and Historical Encyclopedia, Volume 2*, retrieved March 19, 2014 from books.google.com/books?id=4X44KbDBl9gC&printsec=frontcover&source=gbs_ge_summary_r&cad=0#v=onepage&q&f=false

Chapter 6: The Government that Came to Stay

p. 47, Locke, *The Second Treatise on Civil Government*.

p. 51, Locke, John, "Book I. Of Government; Chapter IX. Of Monarchy by Inheritance from Adam," retrieved March 19, 2014 from www.bartleby.com/169/109.html

p. 54, "The Maryland Toleration Act 1649," retrieved March 19, 2014 from www.let.rug.nl/usa/documents/1600-1650/the-maryland-toleration-act-1649.php

p. 55, Penn, William, *The Fruits of Solitude*, retrieved March 19, 2014 from www.bartleby.com/1/3/170.html

p. 55, Penn, William, "Pennsylvania Charter of Privileges," retrieved March 19, 2014 from www.ushistory.org/penn/quotes.htm

Chapter 7: By the People

p. 65, "Massachusetts Body of Liberties, 1641," retrieved March 19, 2014 from www.constitution.org/bcp/mabodlib.htm

Index

Page numbers in **boldface** are images.

absolute monarchs, 9
Age of Exploration, 10, 14
Americas, the, 5, 35–37, 45
aristocracy, 9–10, 18, 64
assembly, 14, 50, **52**

Biblical law, 61
Boston Tea Party, 33

charters, 13, **22**, 23–25, 27
checks and balances, 19
commoners, 7, 12
commonwealth, 29, 59–60, 65
confederacy, 7
constitution, 9,14, 18–19, 23, 30,
    32, 54, 66
council, 6–7, 24, 27, 43–44

English Bill of Rights, 18
English common laws, 17, 63, 65
Enlightenment, 19, 36, 50, 66

friars, 39–41
Fundamental Orders, 29,
    31–32, **31**

gentry, 9, 18
governor, 7, 25, 32, 36, 40,
    43–44, 50

indentured servants, 29, 32, 44,
    48, 50
Intolerable Acts, **64**, 65

jury, 18, 63
justices of the peace, 61

legislature, 18, 50, 61

magistrates, 31, 33, 43, 45, 61
Magna Carta, **16**, 17–18, 23,
    27, 50
Mayflower, **28**, 29–32, 36
Mayflower Compact,
    30–32, 36
mission, 34, 39–42, **41–42**

monarchs, 5, **8**, 10–12, 17–19,
    23–24, 27, 36–37, 45, 47,
    50, 59, 63
    See also, absolute monarchs
monopolies, 13

New World, 4–5, 10, 12–14,
    23–24, 35–36, 47, 50

Old Testament, 65
Old World, 4, 7, 9–10, 13, 15,
    23, 27

Parliament, 18, 27, 50
    English Parliament, 59,
        63, 66
peasant, 9
peers, 17
Penn, William, 54–55, **54**
Petition of Right, 18, 23,
    27, 50
proprietors, 50, 57

reason, 14, 19, 40, 47–48,
    51, 54
republic, 14

separation of powers, 19, 36
slave codes, 60
Spanish Borderlands, 35–37,
    39–41, 43–44
sponsors, 23

theocracies, 51
town meetings, 60

viceroys, 36–37, 40, 43–44

Author Biography

L. H. Colligan regularly visited her former hometown's colonial era sites and enjoyed traveling back to that period with her family. She has also time travelled to Jamestown, Williamsburg, Charleston, Plymouth, Deerfield, Philadelphia, Albuquerque, and Santa Fe. When driving, she will pull off the road for any burial ground that is at least a few hundred years old. Now a New Englander, she lives within biking distance of two colonial-era town commons. She is grateful, however, for the modern convenience of her computer and Kindle, which have helped her research the many nonfiction books she has written in science, health, history, and literature.